EXPLORING WITH SCIENCE

BY DONNA LONGO

Editorial Offices: Glenview, Illinois • Parsippany, New Jersey • New York, New York
Sales Offices: Needham, Massachusetts • Duluth, Georgia • Glenview, Illinois
Coppell, Texas • Ontario, California • Mesa, Arizona

ISBN: 0-328-13566-6

4 5 6 7 8 9 10 V0G1 14 13 12 11 10 09 08 07 06

AT THE SUMMIT

You are on top of the world! Standing at the summit of Mount Everest, you are on top of the world's tallest mountain. Your climb has been tough. You carried on through snow blindness, little oxygen, and extreme tiredness. You push aside your oxygen mask and smile at your victory.

Due to the lack of oxygen, climbers use oxygen tanks to breathe at high altitudes.

THE WORLD'S HIGHEST MOUNTAIN

Mount Everest was named in honor of Sir George Everest. He created maps of India and the Himalaya Mountains, where Mount Everest stands.

In 1953, Sir Edmund Hillary and Tenzing Norgay became the first people to reach the top of Mount Everest. Since that time, more than 1,300 climbers have made it to the top. In 1956, scientists measured the mountain for the first time. They estimate its height at 29,028 feet (8,847 meters) high.

There are many reasons why climbing Mount Everest is challenging. First, there is little oxygen at such a great height. The mountain is also very steep and has several deep, dangerous cracks. Avalanches are another great danger. They are unexpected and overpowering, and their heavy **debris** can be fatal.

Then there's the weather. Fierce winds and bitterly cold temperatures mean a chance of frostbite. Temperatures can fall to -50° Fahrenheit. Winds can whip at 120 miles per hour.

THE WORLD'S HIGHEST MOUNTAINS

The list below includes the world's ten highest mountains. Each rises higher than 26,248 ft. (8,000 m) above sea level. Look at the height of Mount Everest. Then compare it to the heights of the other mountains.

Everest......................	29,035 ft. (8,850 m)	Cho Oyu	26,906 ft. (8,201 m)
K2 (Godwin Austen).....	28,251 ft. (8,611 m)	Dhaulagiri................	26,795 ft. (8,167 m)
Kangchenjunga	28,169 ft. (8,586 m)	Manaslu	26,781 ft. (8,163 m)
Lhotse......................	27,890 ft. (8,501 m)	Nanga Parbat...........	26,795 ft. (8,167 m)
Makalu....................	26,781 ft. (8,163 m)	Annapurna..............	26,545 ft. (8,091 m)

THEN AND NOW

When Sir Edmund Hillary reached the top of Mount Everest, he did his own measuring. He found it to be 29,000 feet high. Since the first measurements were taken, there have been major advances in science. New measurements were taken in 1999 using this new science. Thanks to satellites orbiting Earth, scientists correctly measured Everest at 8,850 meters (29,035 feet).

How did they do it? Professor Bradford Washburn used radar and global positioning satellites (GPS). The new high-tech equipment was light—less than forty-two pounds. It was broken down into four pieces, so four people carried its parts to the top of Mount Everest.

Now people use GPS units in their cars. These devices tell drivers exactly where they are, and they can tell the driver the best way to get somewhere.

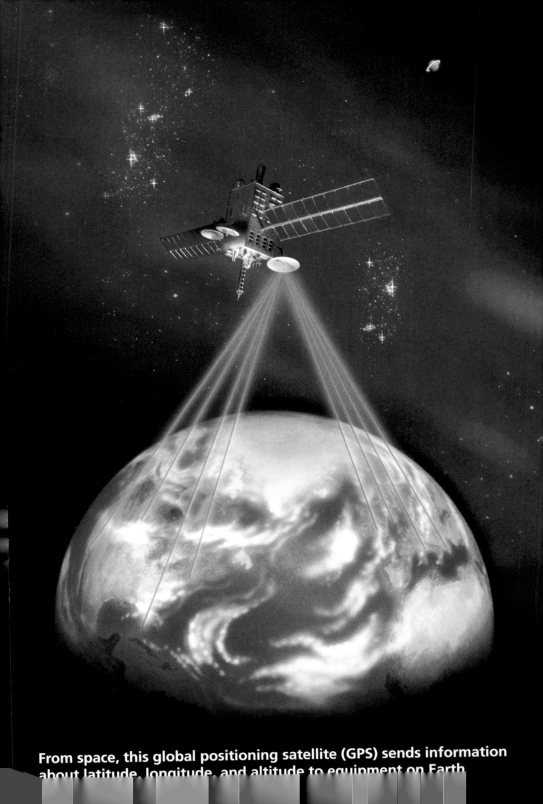

From space, this global positioning satellite (GPS) sends information about latitude, longitude, and altitude to equipment on Earth.

CALL OR E-MAIL FROM MOUNT EVEREST

When Sir Edmund Hillary and Tenzing Norgay first reached Mount Everest, it took days before their big news reached the rest of the world. Times have changed. Advances in science help people communicate from the top of the world by satellite telephone.

Scientists and climbers depend on satellite phones on Mount Everest. Photographers and journalists use them to help us learn more about the mountain.

What are satellite telephones? They are also called "sat phones," or "satellite terminals." As their name suggests, they use satellite technology. There are several satellites now orbiting Earth. Sat phones send signals to these satellites. They also receive signals from them. Standing at the top of the world, a joyous adventurer can call just about anyone on Earth to share the goods news.

A satellite telephone allows people to make calls from the most remote places.

How would you like to get an e-mail from Mount Everest? Sat phones make that possible too. Explorers and scientists have sent e-mails to co-workers, family, friends, and students waiting eagerly for news. Digital pictures, audio messages, and videos can also be sent using sat phones.

HAND-HELD TECHNOLOGY

You have learned about the satellites in orbit around Earth. They help us learn about and communicate from Mount Everest. What other tools help those who explore the mountain?

An important part of mountain climbing is knowing where you are. A hand-held GPS device can help. This light and portable device allows climbers to figure out their location on the mountain. Climbers also need to know their altitude as they climb. An altimeter shows height above sea level. A small altimeter can be worn like a watch. It includes a barometer to track changes in the weather.

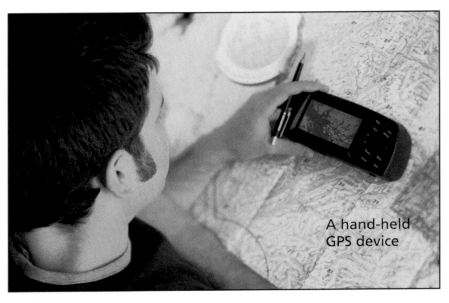

A hand-held GPS device

An altimeter

Braving the Elements

When climbing to extremely high altitudes, people must be careful. They must slowly get used to the lower levels of oxygen. This is called "acclimatization." The change to a new height takes place over several days. In time, the body adjusts to less oxygen. What happens when someone climbs too high too quickly? Acute Mountain Sickness (AMS) can happen.

It can be hard to take care of a sick person in such a remote place as Mount Everest. With new technology, AMS can be treated with a Gamow Bag. This portable pressurization chamber was invented by Igor Gamow. Inside its **cramped** quarters, a climber can recover from AMS.

Most people think of technology as electronics. But technology can be a new tool or material too. New technology allows people to create lighter, warmer, drier clothing for mountain climbers.

At such a high altitude, it is important to stay warm. The cold carries great dangers. These include severe frostbite. New synthetic materials are lightweight and warm. Facing bitter cold, climbers depend on a synthetic protective wind suit.

A Gamow Bag provides the pressure necessary to recover from AMS.

ON TO ANTARCTICA!

Now that you have conquered Everest, you are off on your next adventure: Antarctica. It has great challenges too. The weather is its greatest test.

Antarctica has been called a desert of ice, the last frontier, the frozen continent, and the unknown land. With its bone-chilling weather and hurricane-force winds, it may be the planet's most uninviting place. Massive icebergs crowd its waters. Gigantic glaciers move across its lands. Coastal areas have summer temperatures of around 50°F (10°C). The **interior** of the continent is frigid. It boasts the world's lowest recorded temperature -128.6°F (-89.2°C). That's why Antarctica is used mainly for research.

In the 1800s, explorers sailed along the coasts of Antarctica. It was not until 1911 that people explored its interior. In a race to reach the South Pole, Roald Amundsen won on December 14, 1911. He used a tool called a sextant to check his latitude and longitude. That way, he could be sure he had reached the pole.

Antarctica is one of the coldest places on Earth.

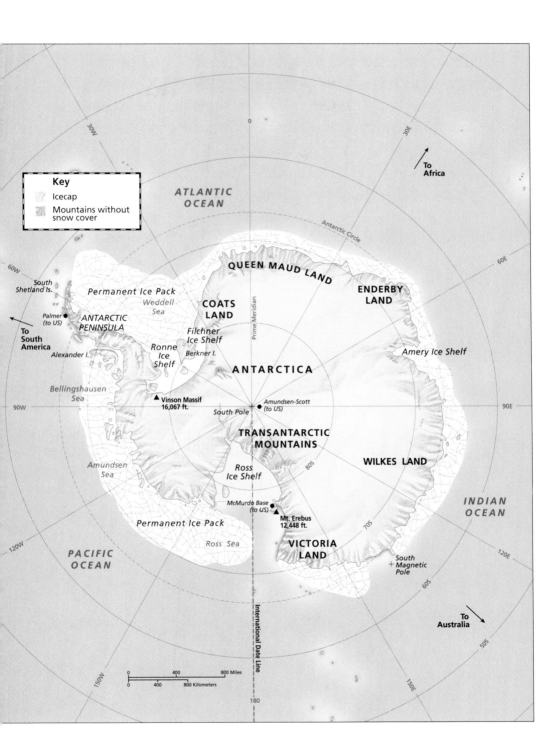

Key
- Icecap
- Mountains without snow cover

ATLANTIC OCEAN

Antarctic Circle

QUEEN MAUD LAND

ENDERBY LAND

30W

0

30E

To Africa

60W

South Shetland Is.

Permanent Ice Pack

Weddell Sea

COATS LAND

Palmer (to US)

ANTARCTIC PENINSULA

Filchner Ice Shelf

Prime Meridian

60E

Amery Ice Shelf

To South America

Ronne Ice Shelf

Berkner I.

Alexander I.

ANTARCTICA

Bellingshausen Sea

90W

▲ Vinson Massif 16,067 ft.

South Pole

Amundsen-Scott (to US)

90E

Amundsen Sea

TRANSANTARCTIC MOUNTAINS

80S

WILKES LAND

INDIAN OCEAN

Ross Ice Shelf

McMurdo Base (to US)

▲ Mt. Erebus 12,448 ft.

70S

Permanent Ice Pack

Ross Sea

VICTORIA LAND

South + Magnetic Pole

120W

PACIFIC OCEAN

120E

60S

International Date Line

150W

150E

50S

0   400   800 Miles
0   400   800 Kilometers

180

To Australia

15

A Research Continent

In the 1950s, Richard Byrd of the U.S. Navy explored the continent by air. Soon, a flurry of scientists headed for Antarctica. By 1959, twelve nations had signed the Antarctic Treaty. It was an agreement that said the continent would be used for research.

The United States's McMurdo Station is one of thirty stations on the continent and its islands. The United States also uses the Palmer Station on Anvers Island and Ross Island's Amundson-Scott South Pole station.

Scientists live at McMurdo Station throughout the year, even during the sunless winter months of June and July. McMurdo Station is home to most of the people on the continent. It's like a very small village with only two hundred tough residents. In the summer, however, more than twelve hundred scientists and researchers live there.

The McMurdo Station is a year-round research center. It is the largest research base in Antarctica.

17

NEW SCIENCE IN THE WATER

What tools do scientists use in the Antarctic? It depends whether their work is on land or in the water.

The hand-held GPS used on Mount Everest comes in handy in Antarctica too. It's not like the sextant that Roald Amundsen used to learn his location. The GPS device communicates with a satellite to find an exact location.

What does a 10-ton killer whale sound like? A hydrophone helps marine biologists find out. The first hydrophones were used to locate submarines and icebergs. A hydrophone works by picking up the sounds that pass through water. It changes them to electromagnetic waves. Now scientists can listen to how marine mammals communicate underwater.

Placing a hydrophone in water

SCIENCE IN WATER AND ON THE ICE

Marine biologists in Antarctica face frosty challenges. To reach the ocean waters, they must drill through six feet of ice. A giant drill digs diving holes into the thick ice.

Underwater, **sonar** finds objects that divers can't see. By bouncing sound waves off objects, sonar measures how far away they are.

Using underwater cameras, marine biologists capture photos of sea stars and sea urchins.

What are scientists studying underwater? As you have seen, some are watching marine life. Others are collecting samples of **sediment** from the **ooze** at the bottom of the sea. It is tough work and it involves hauling pails of mud through the water.

Under the ice, these biologists remove samples of plankton to study. These tiny animals and plants supply food for fish and other marine life.

RADIO TRANSMITTERS

Biologists are studying the emperor penguins of Antarctica. They want to learn more about the places where penguins feed at sea. They track their movements with radio transmitters, which they attach to penguins. The transmitters send out radio waves. Using an antenna, headphones, and a receiver, a scientist can listen to the signals from the transmitters.

TIME TO HEAD HOME

Now it's time to head for home. All the technology you have seen has encouraged you to keep working on a **robotic** drill you're building to take back to Antarctica on your next visit!

Sea stars and sea urchins

Planning a Satellite Launch

Suppose you were looking over the shoulder of a scientist who is gathering a team to launch a new satellite. You see the group has chosen Antarctica as the launch site. The goal is to measure heat radiation on Earth's surface. Before setting out for Antarctica, the scientists need to make some plans.

The Team

First, the head scientist posts announcements to find the right team members, including meteorologists, geologists, and physicists. They must meet these qualifications:

- understand world exploration charts
- know radar topography for showing mountains, valleys, rivers, forests of Earth's surface
- have experience at mountaineering

The Clothing

At McMurdo Station in Antarctica, team members will need extreme weather gear (EWG) including the following:

- fleece jackets
- a cap called a "yazoo" that has a warm inner layer
- a gaiter for the neck (very important)
- bibbed polar pants

The Technology

Some of the tools used in satellite work are as follows:

- 3-D maps for Earth observation
- weather satellites for measuring cloud patterns or air pollution
- TV and telephone signals; radio relays for communication
- navigation tools

After the plans are made and the tents are set up, the real work begins—observing Earth!

Glossary

cramped *adj.* tightly crowded and close together.

debris *n.* pieces of broken materials, scattered over an area.

interior *n.* the inside of a structure or land mass.

ooze *n.* very soft mud or slime, especially at the bottom of a body of water.

robotic *adj.* mechanized or computerized.

sediment *n.* material that settles at the bottom of a liquid.

sonar *n.* a device that uses sound waves to locate objects underwater or to determine how deep water is.